LEARN ABOUT PAGANISM

Samhain
WITH
Grani Hulda

Pagan Books for Pagan Kids
Grani Hulda

This book belongs to:

_____

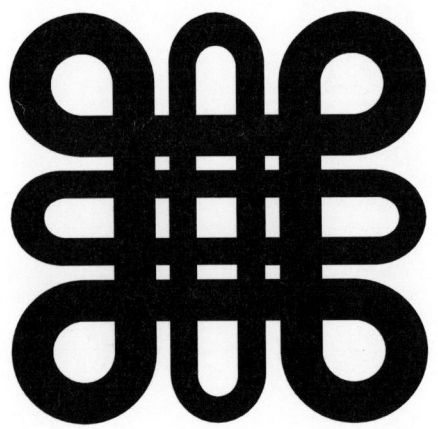

2022 Grani Hulda

What is Samhain?

Samhain is a holy day celebrated by Pagans around the world. It is celebrated halfway between Fall and Winter.

At Samhain, leaves fall from trees. Change is happening.

Samhain symbols remind us that we do not live forever. Death is a normal part of the cycle of life, just like being born is.

Samhain is a powerful spiritual holiday. We celebrate the people that have passed on from this life.

As the Earth changes from summer to winter, plants die. Birds fly south for the winter.

Some animals go to sleep for the winter. Bears, skunks and bats hibernate. Squirrels and mice snuggle into their nests.

A lot of fairies also hibernate.

Grani Hulda has put her garden to bed for the winter, too.

The Witches' New Year

Samhain is sometimes known as the Witches' New Year.

The Witches' New Year is a time to create magic spells and potions.

Witches meet up with other witches at Samhain to create more powerful magic together.

Samhain marks the end of the harvest and that is something to celebrate!

Celebrate Samhain

There are many ways to celebrate Samhain.

Samhain is a good time to make a memory table for loved ones who have passed away. Decorate it with pretty objects and photos.

Grani Hulda likes to celebrate Samhain at the nearest Full Moon.

Grani Hulda celebrates Samhain by making a list of changes that she wants to make in her life. She burns her list in a Samhain fire.

Samhain is a good time to make a list of things you want in your life. Grani Hulda also makes a list of books to read.

Winter is a good time to dream. Grani Hulda will have a lot of ideas for her life by the time Spring comes.

Samhain is a good time to make crafts. Grani Hulda likes to carve a pumpkin and make other Samhain decorations.

Grani Hulda also makes tiny fairy beds at Samhain. She hides them around the yard so that the fairies can use them during the long, dark winter.

Grani Hulda takes a walk in the cold, autumn air and sings a goodbye song to Summer.

Printed in Great Britain
by Amazon